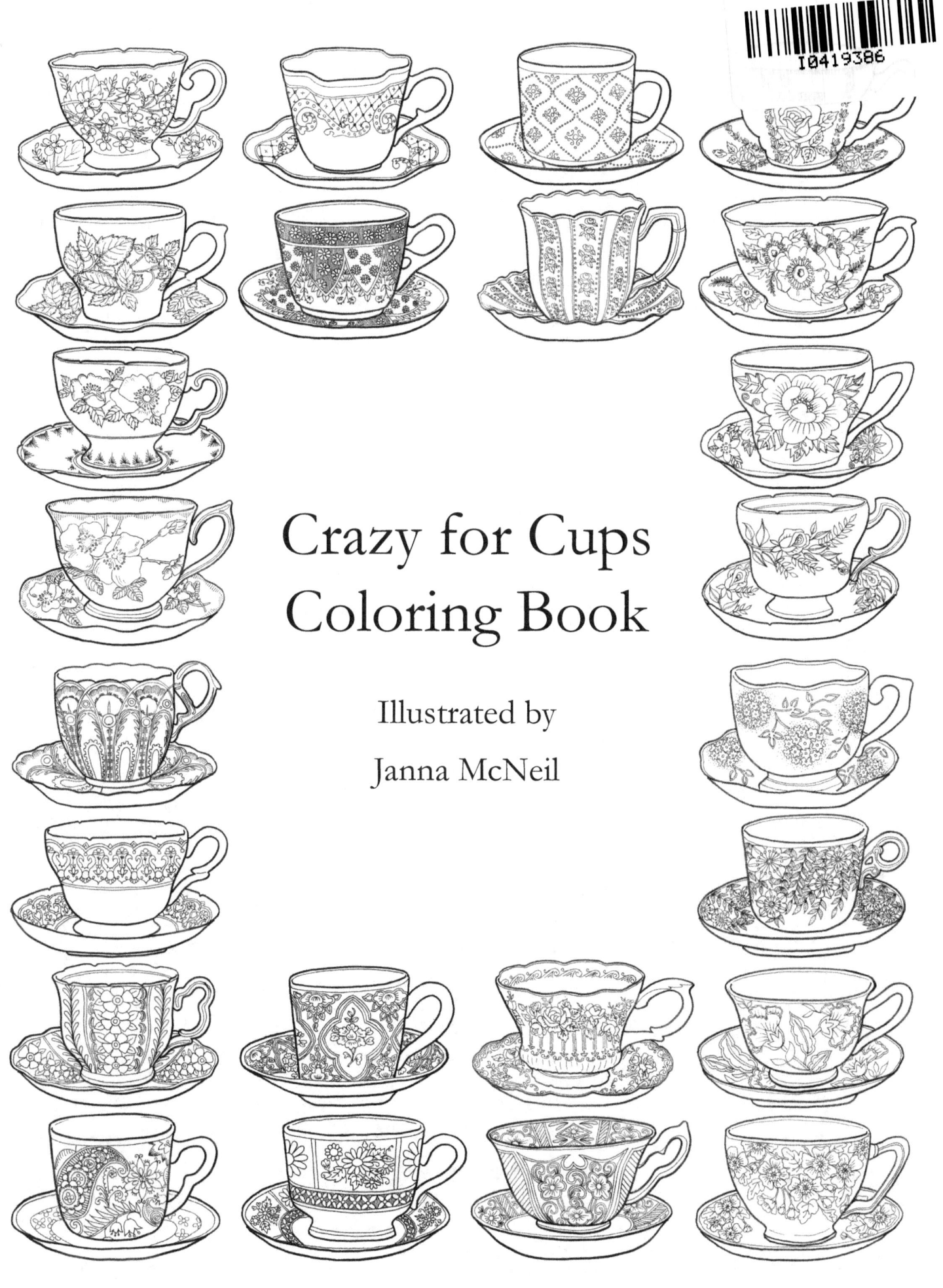

Crazy for Cups
Coloring Book

Illustrated by

Janna McNeil

ABOUT THE ARTIST

Janna McNeil [Canadian, 1975-] is a self-taught artist based in Northborough, Massachusetts. Her hand drawn designs are inspired by antique and vintage tea cups from around the world.

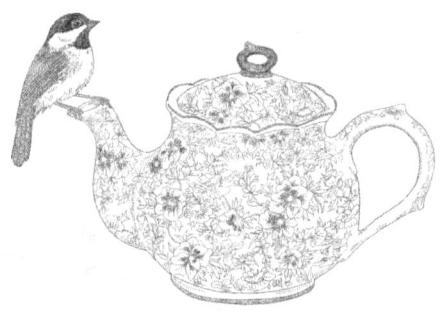

ISBN: 1720509093
ISBN-13: 978-1720509097

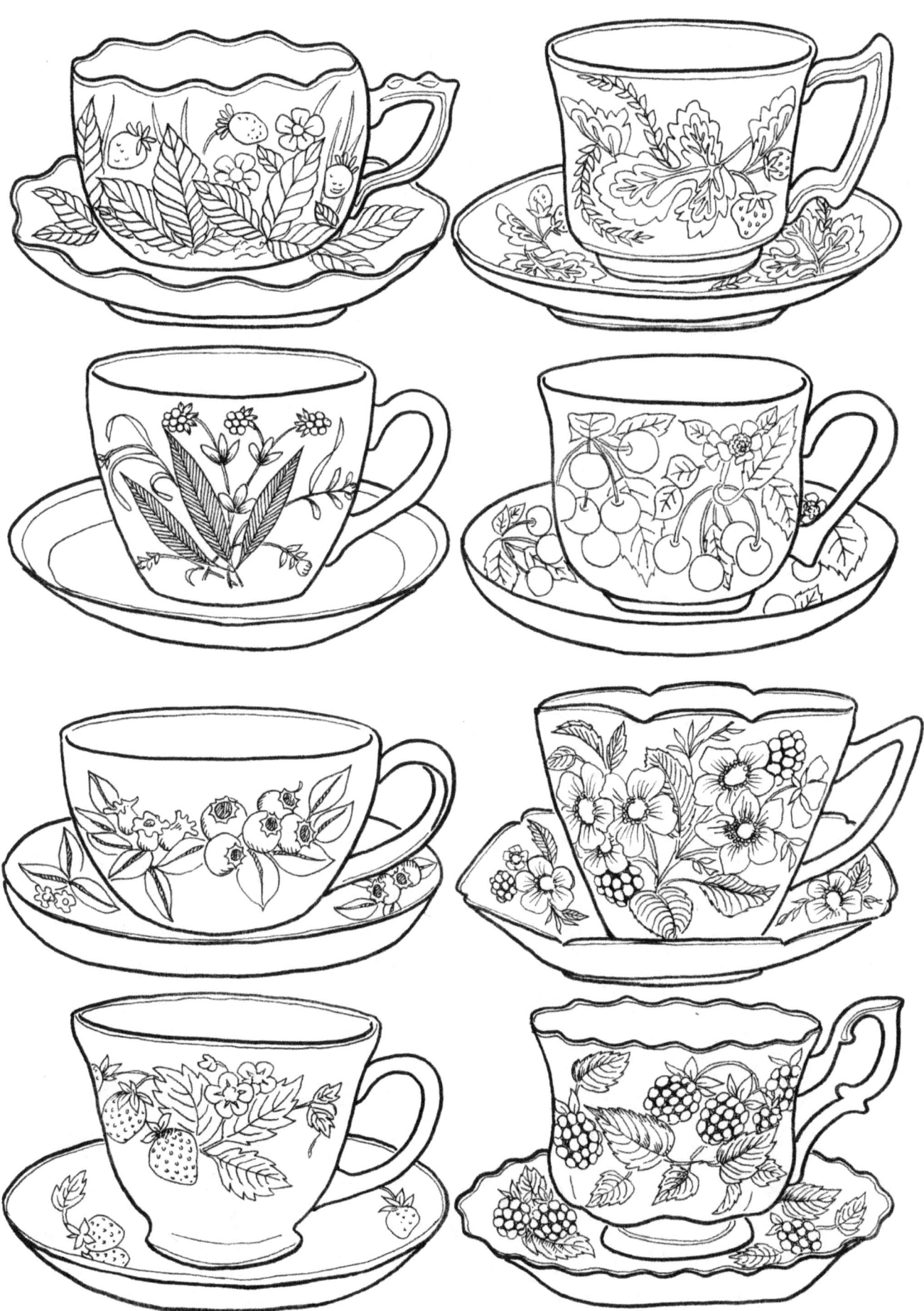

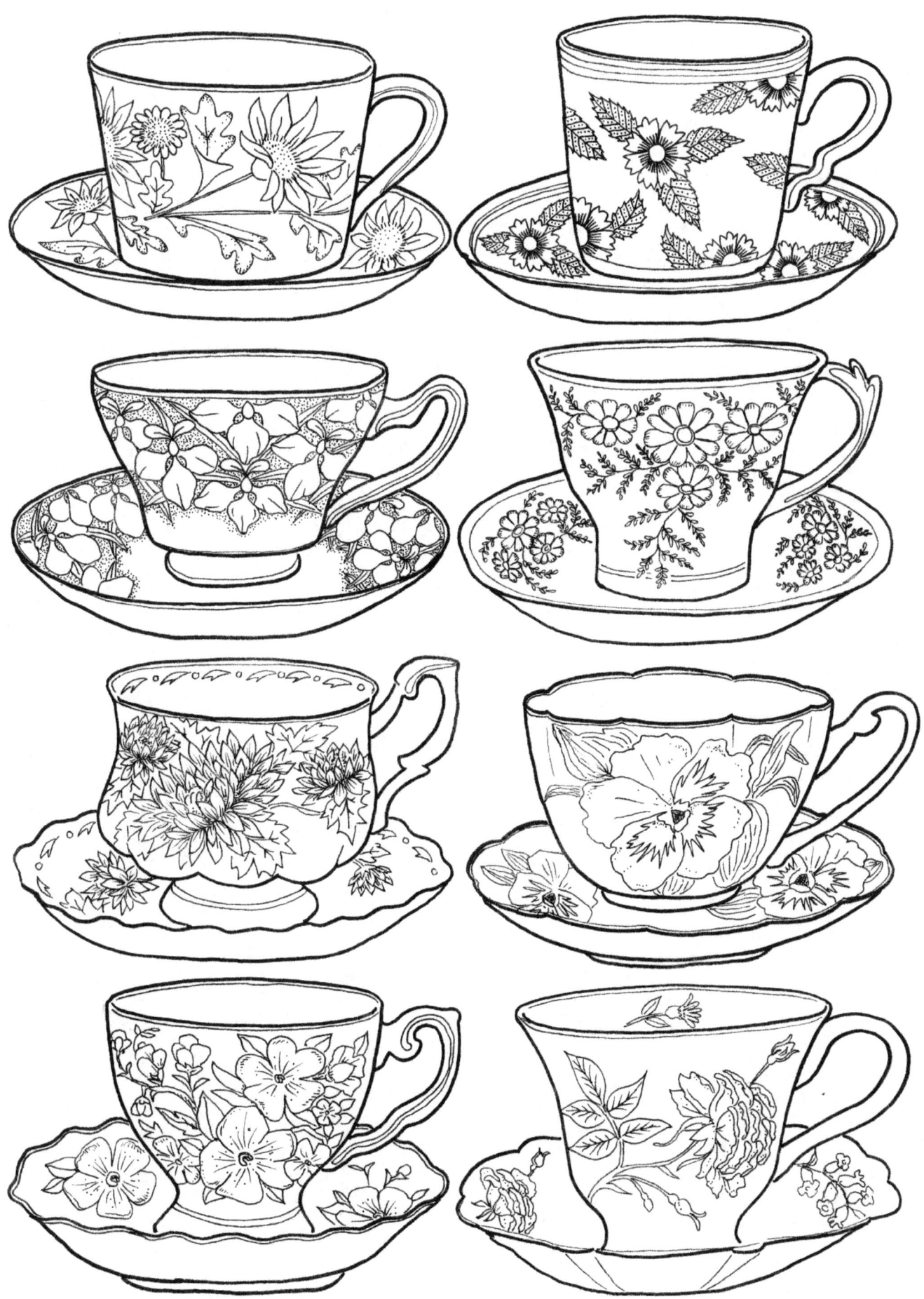

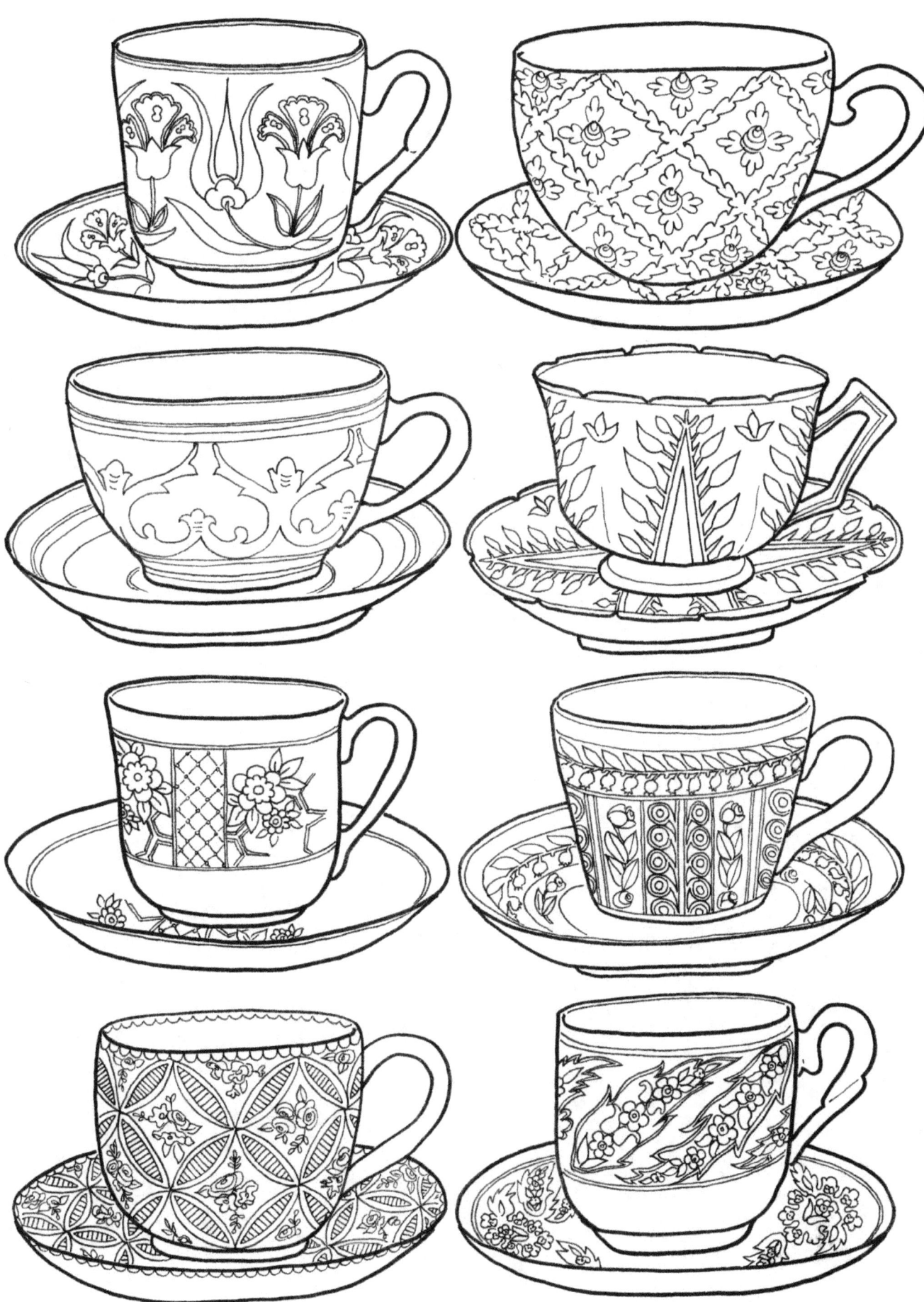

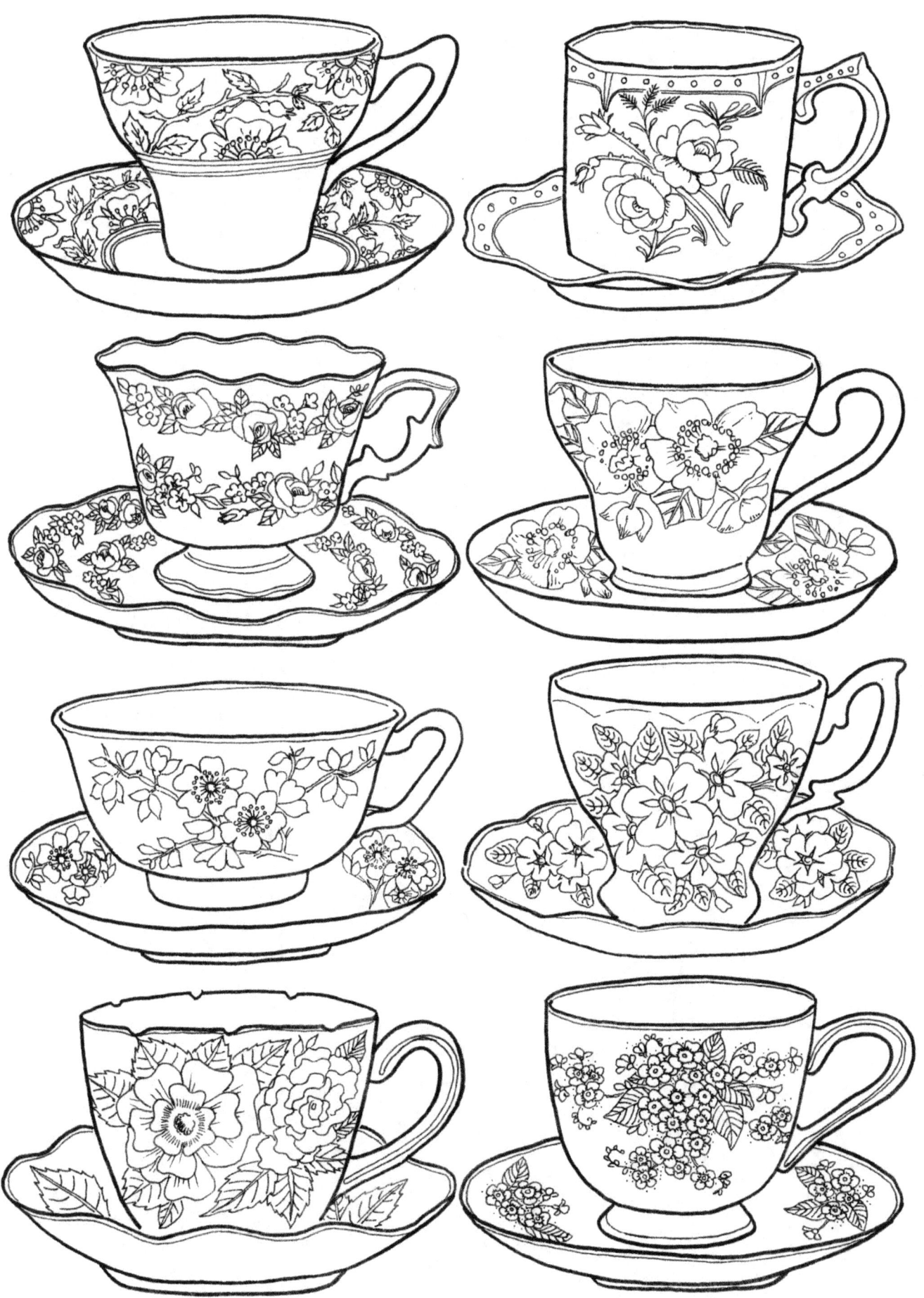

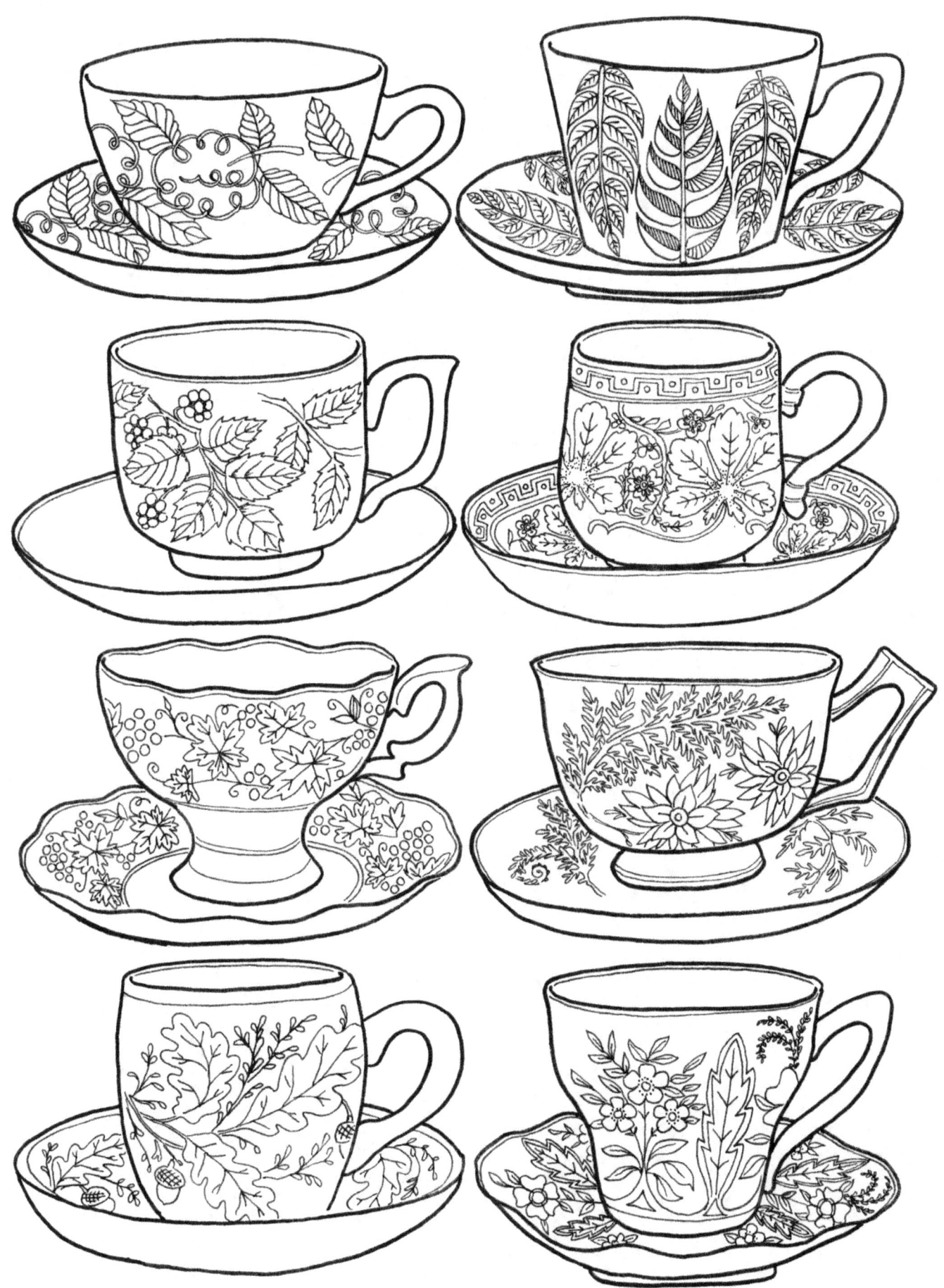

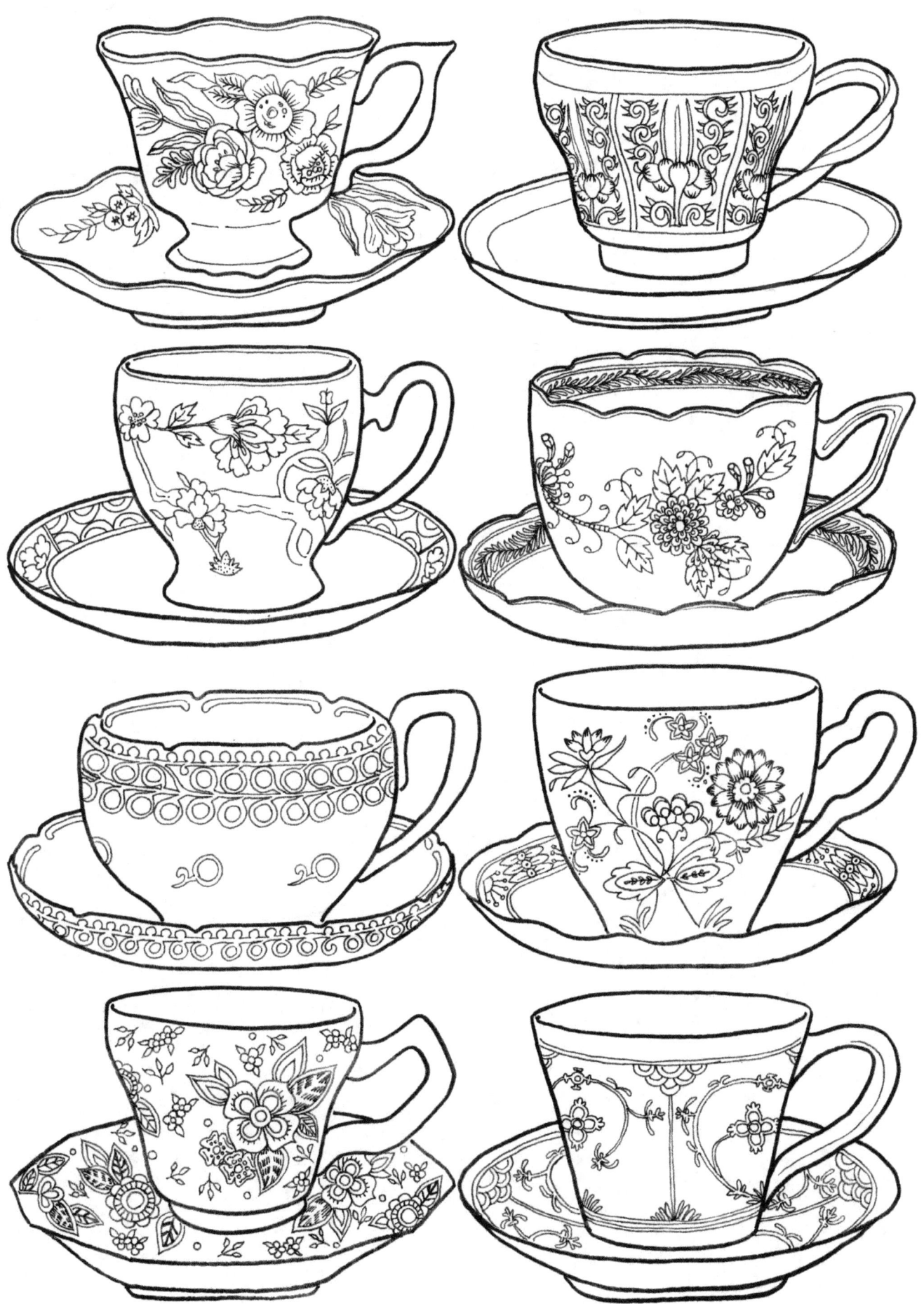

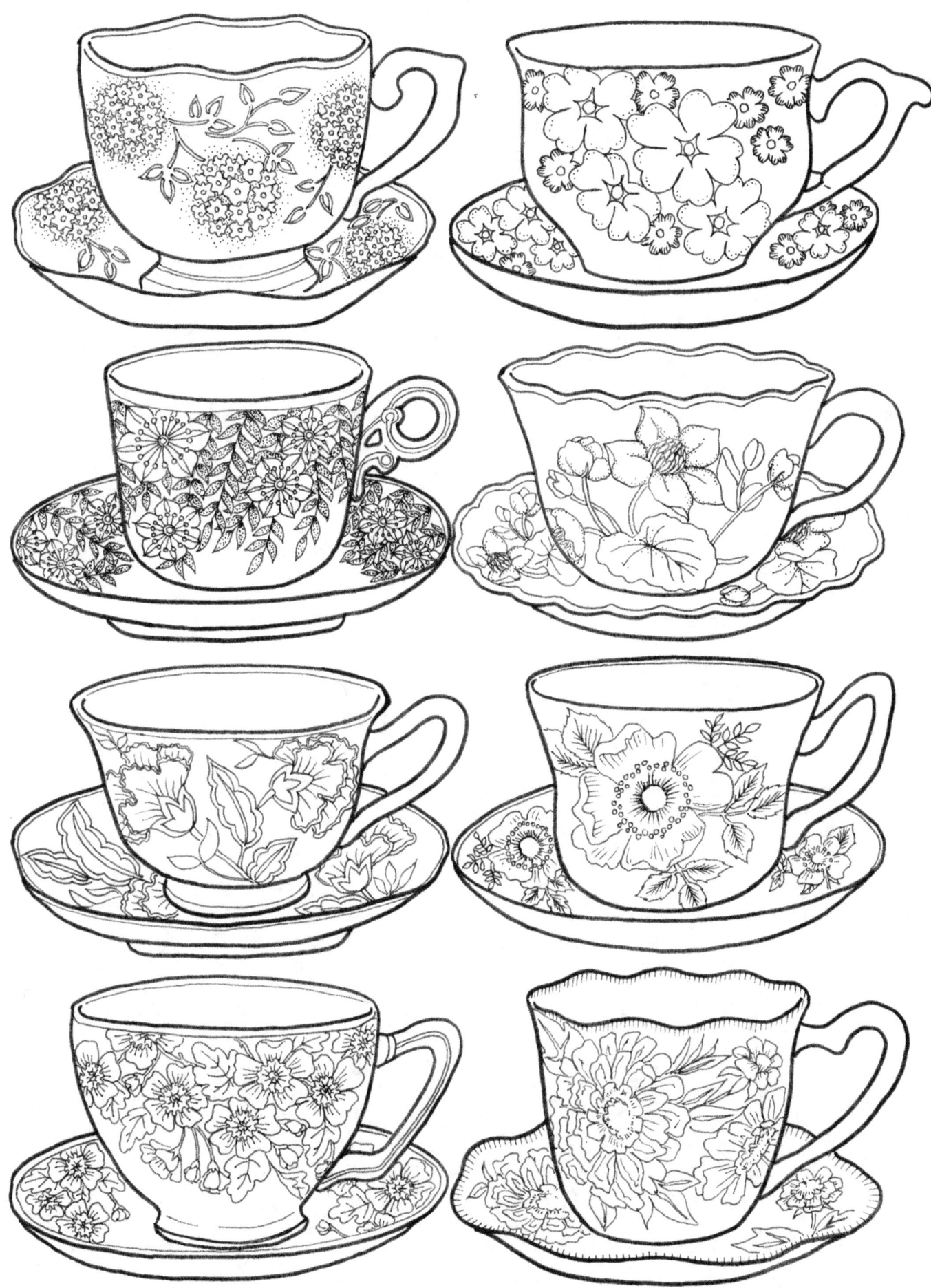

13

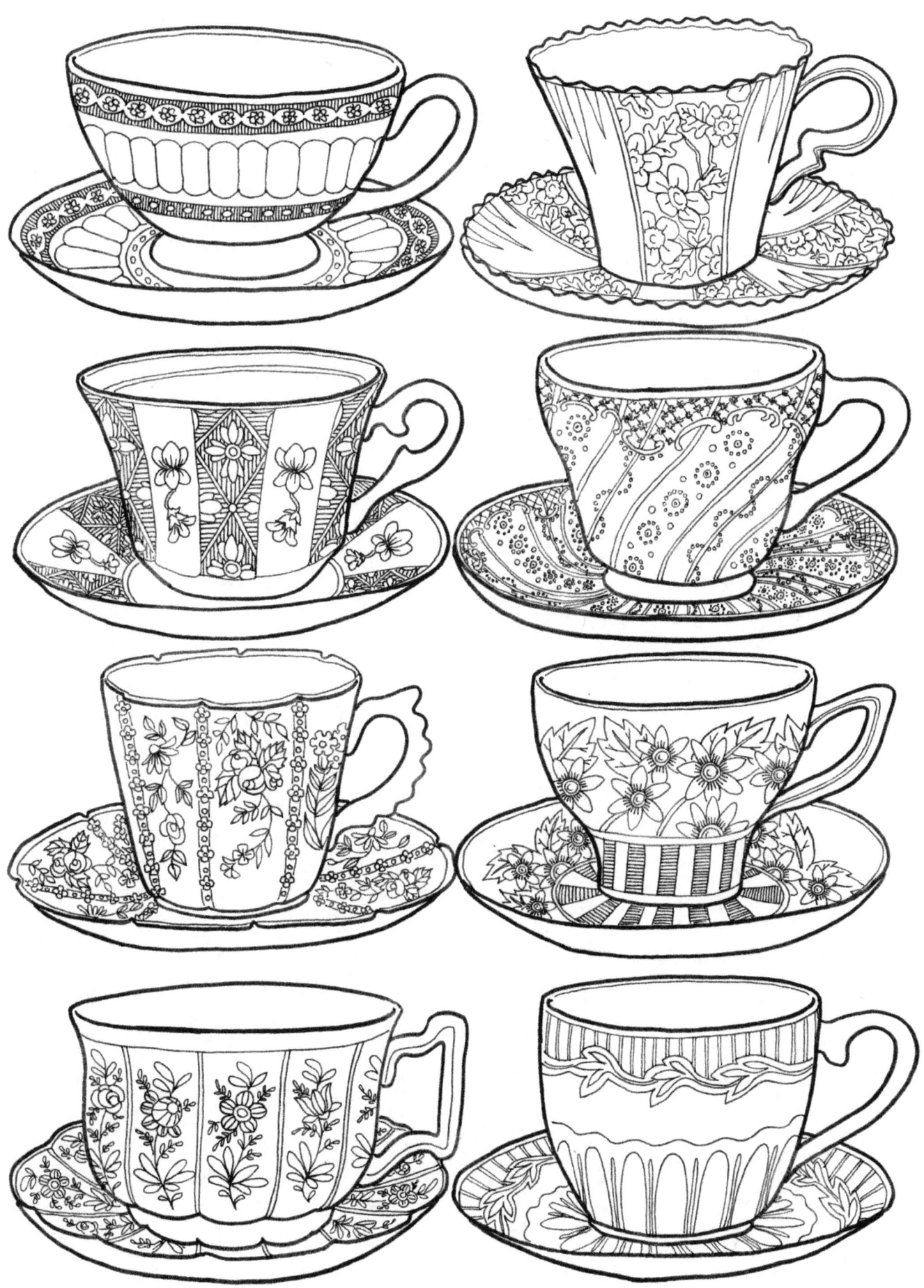

Janna McNeil

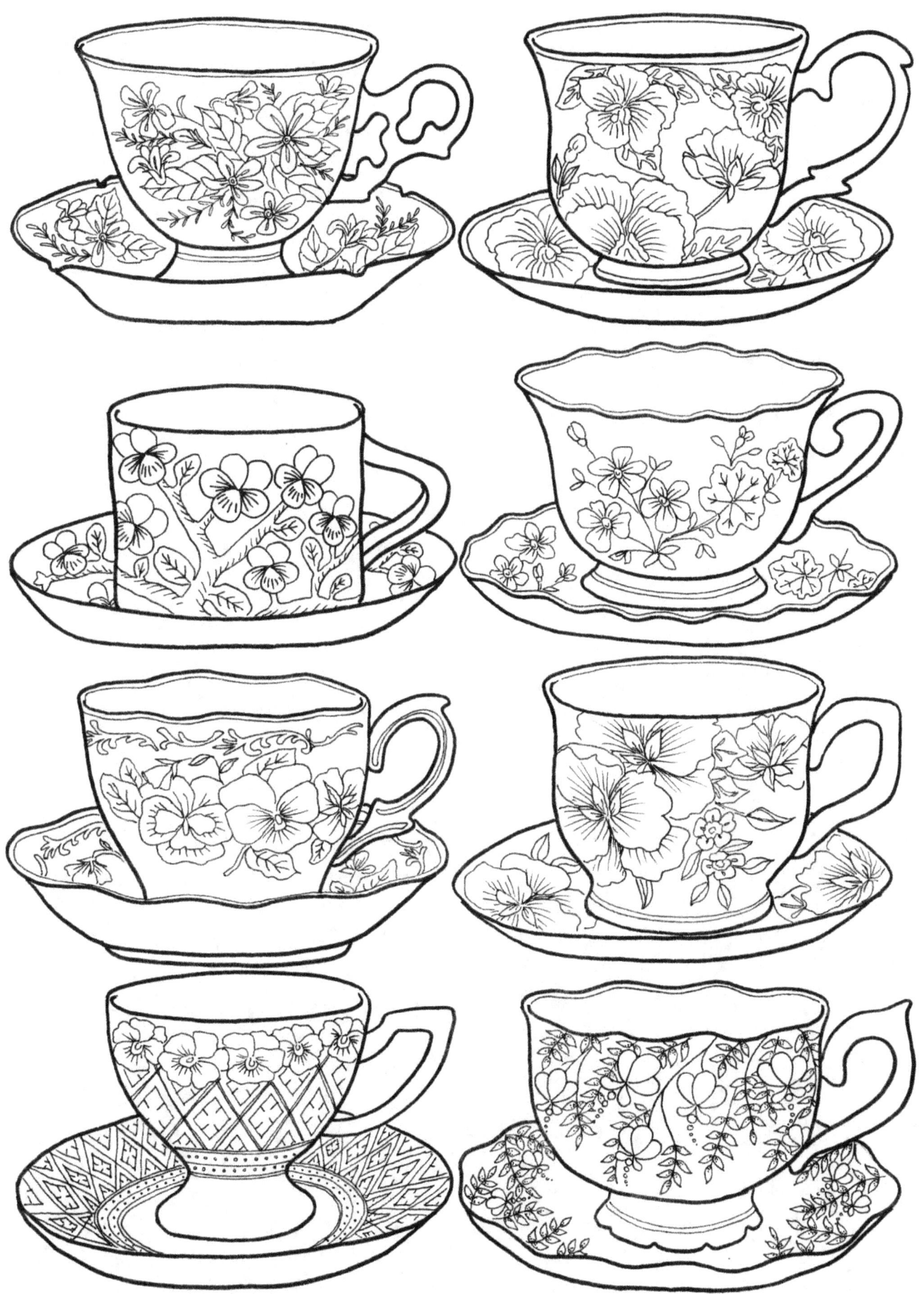

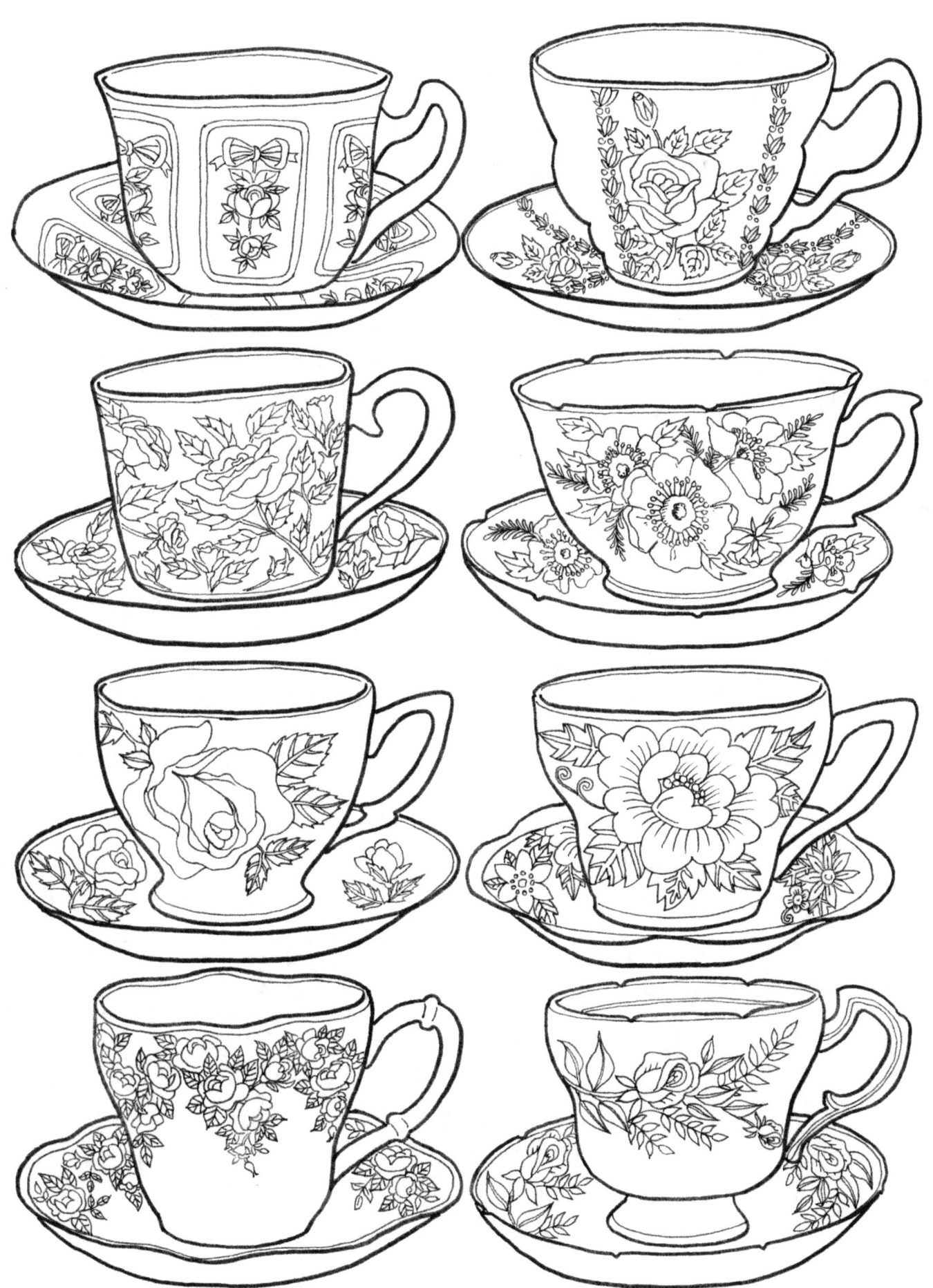

19

Janna McNeil

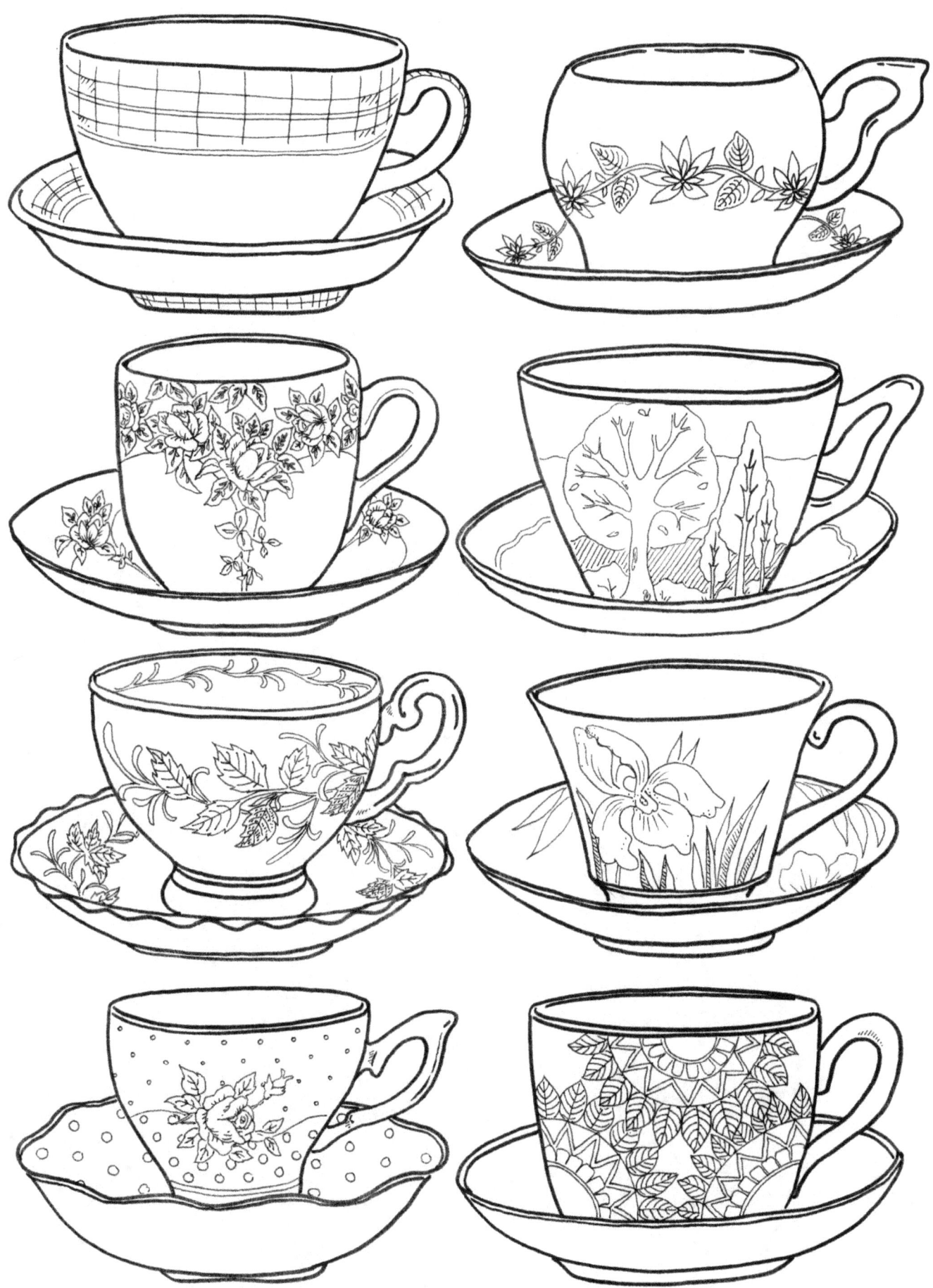

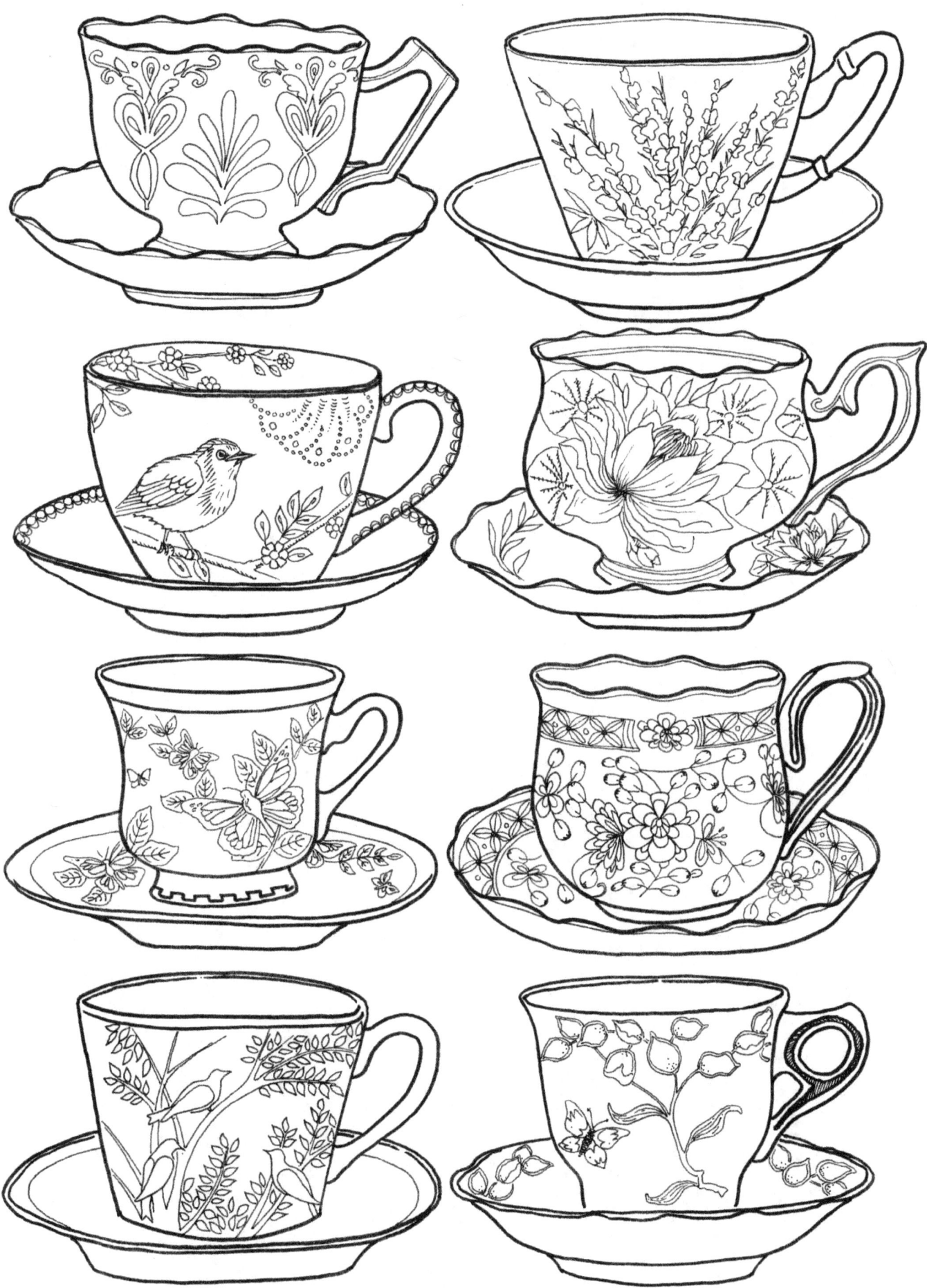

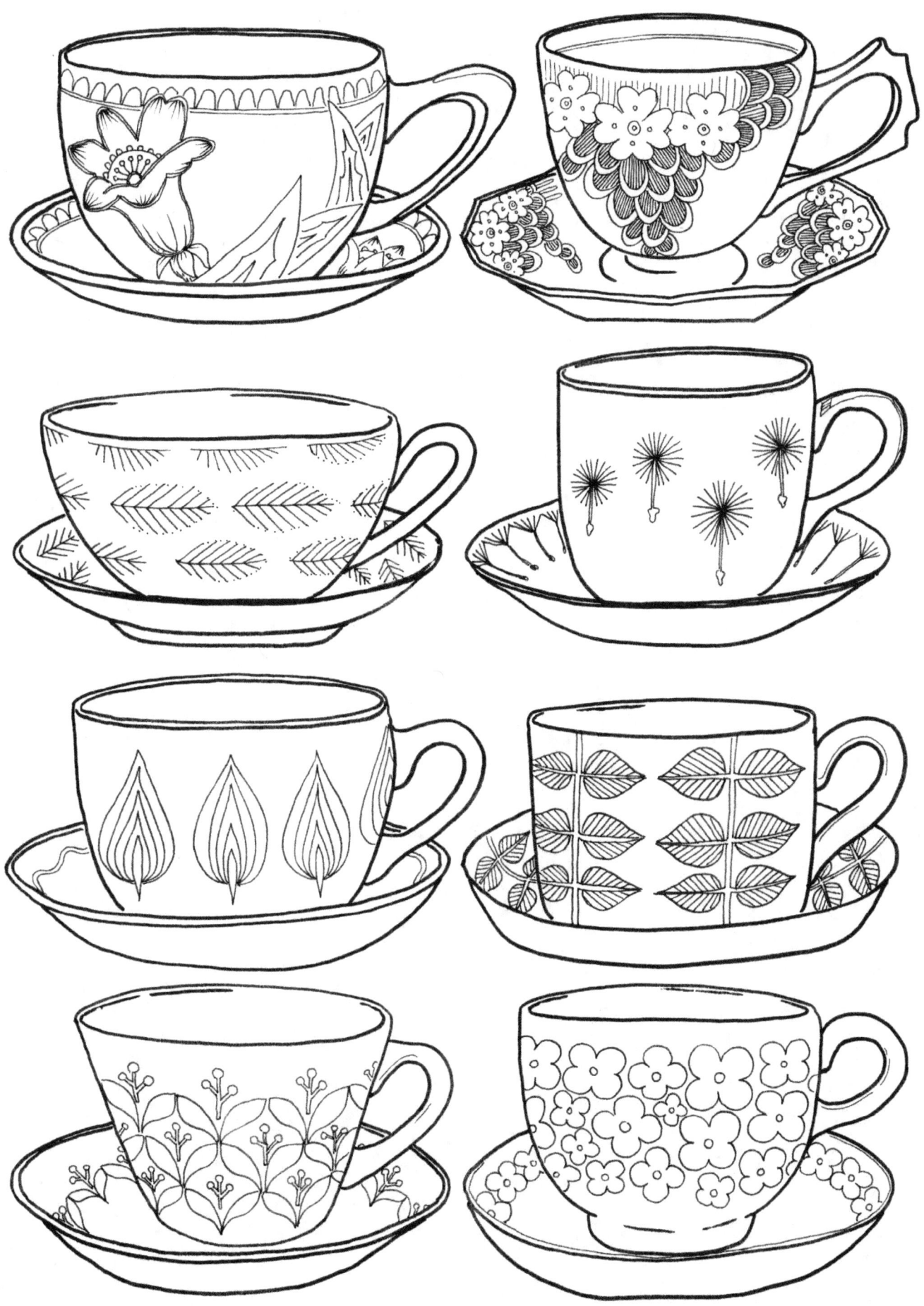

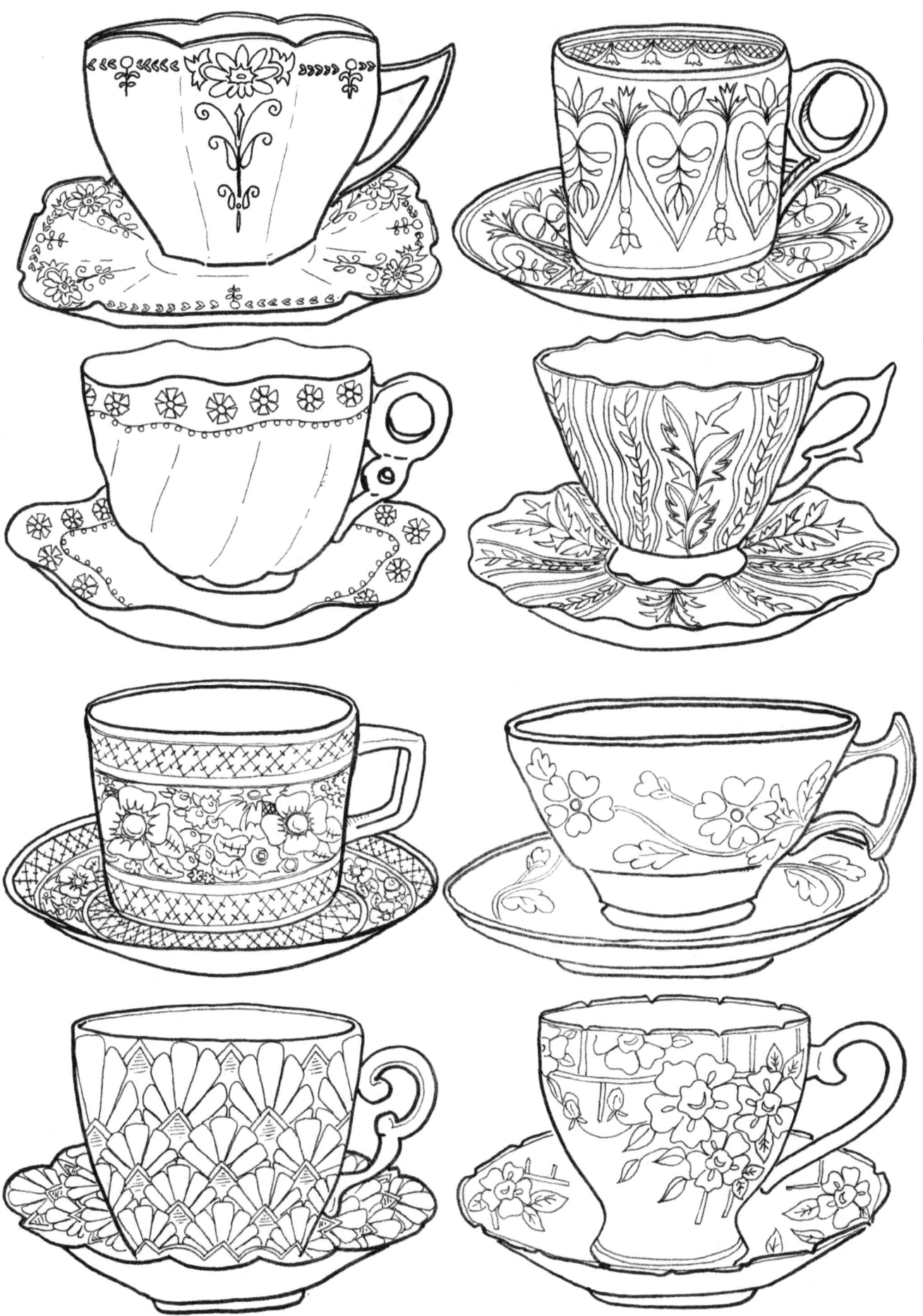

29

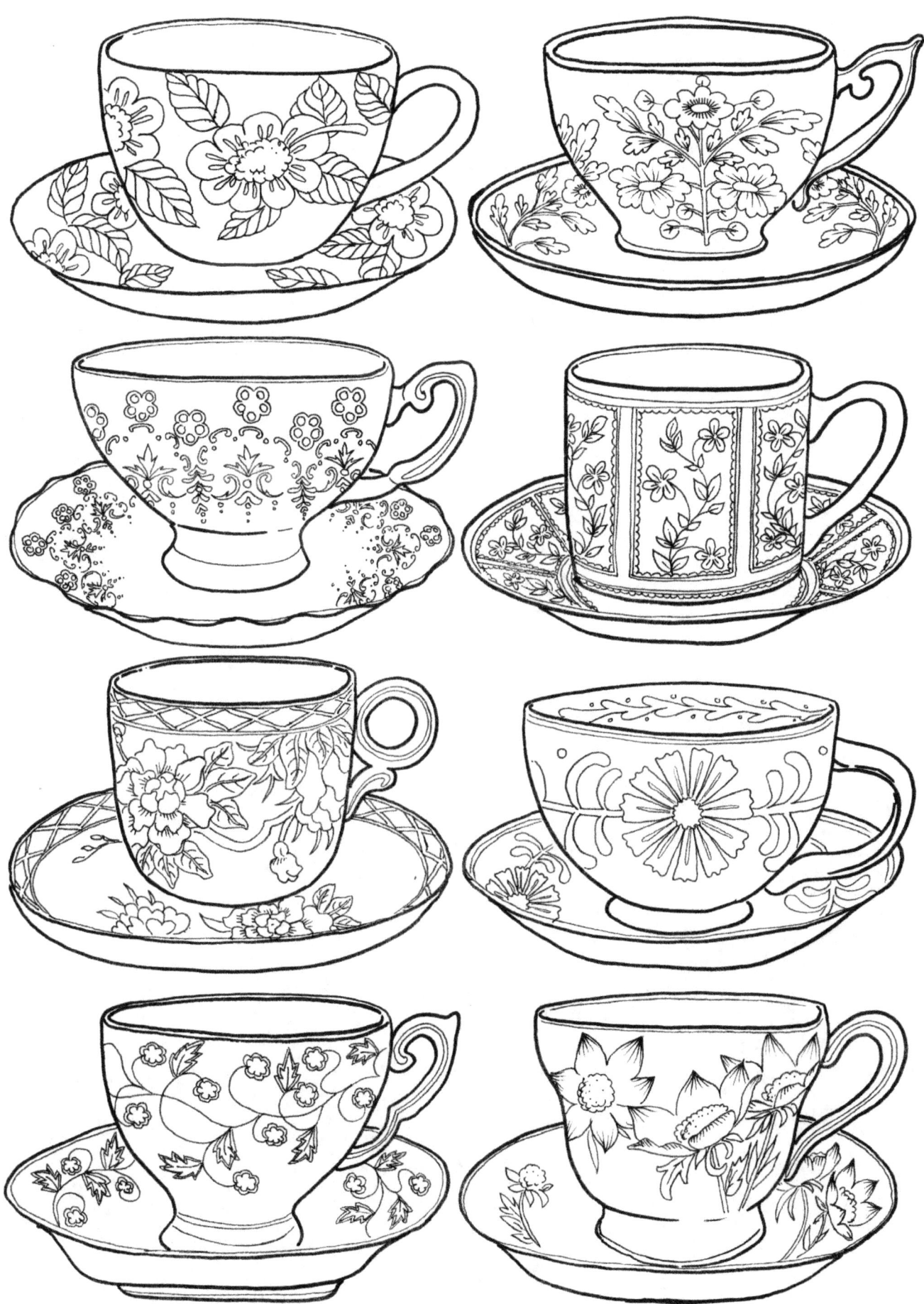

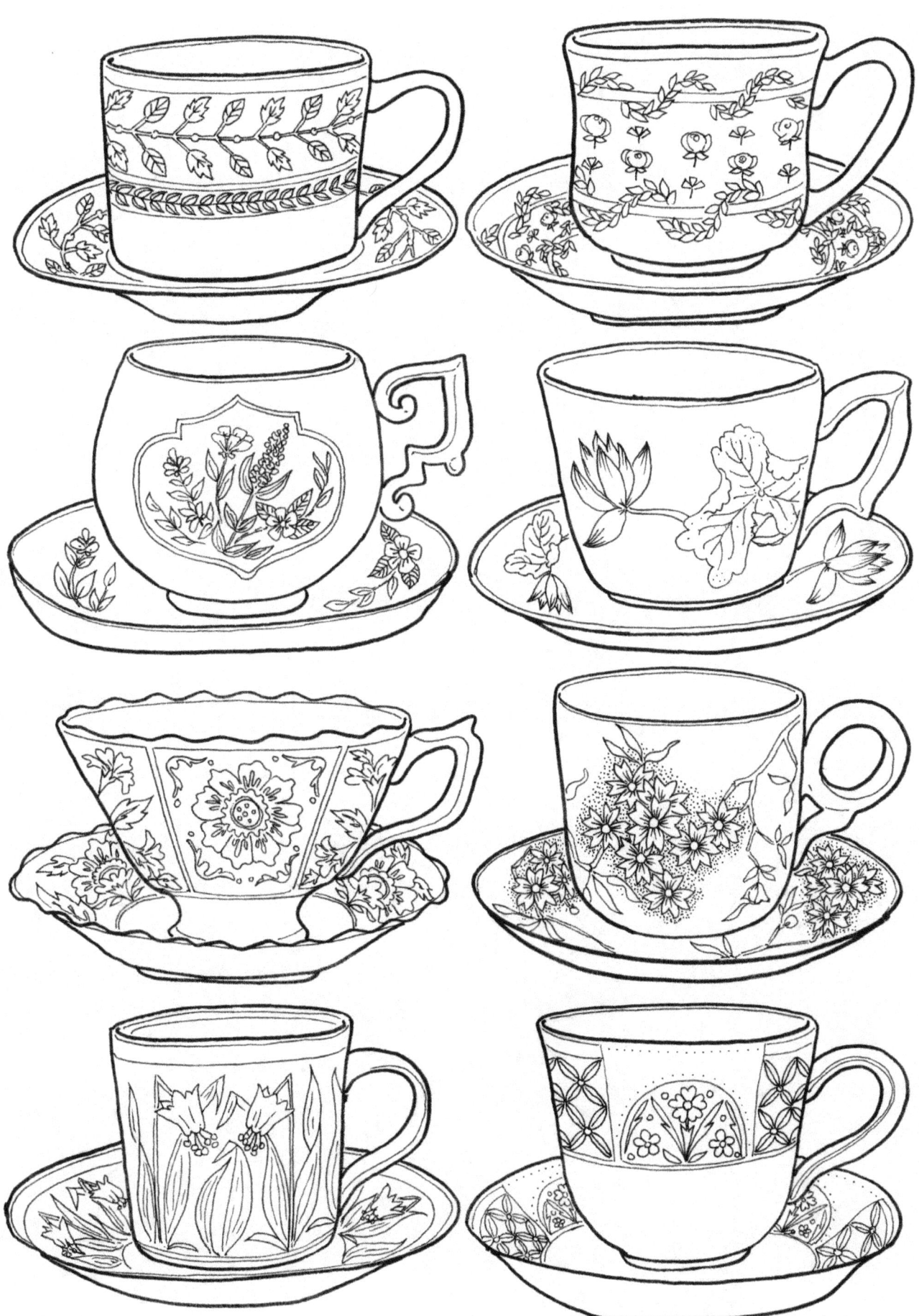

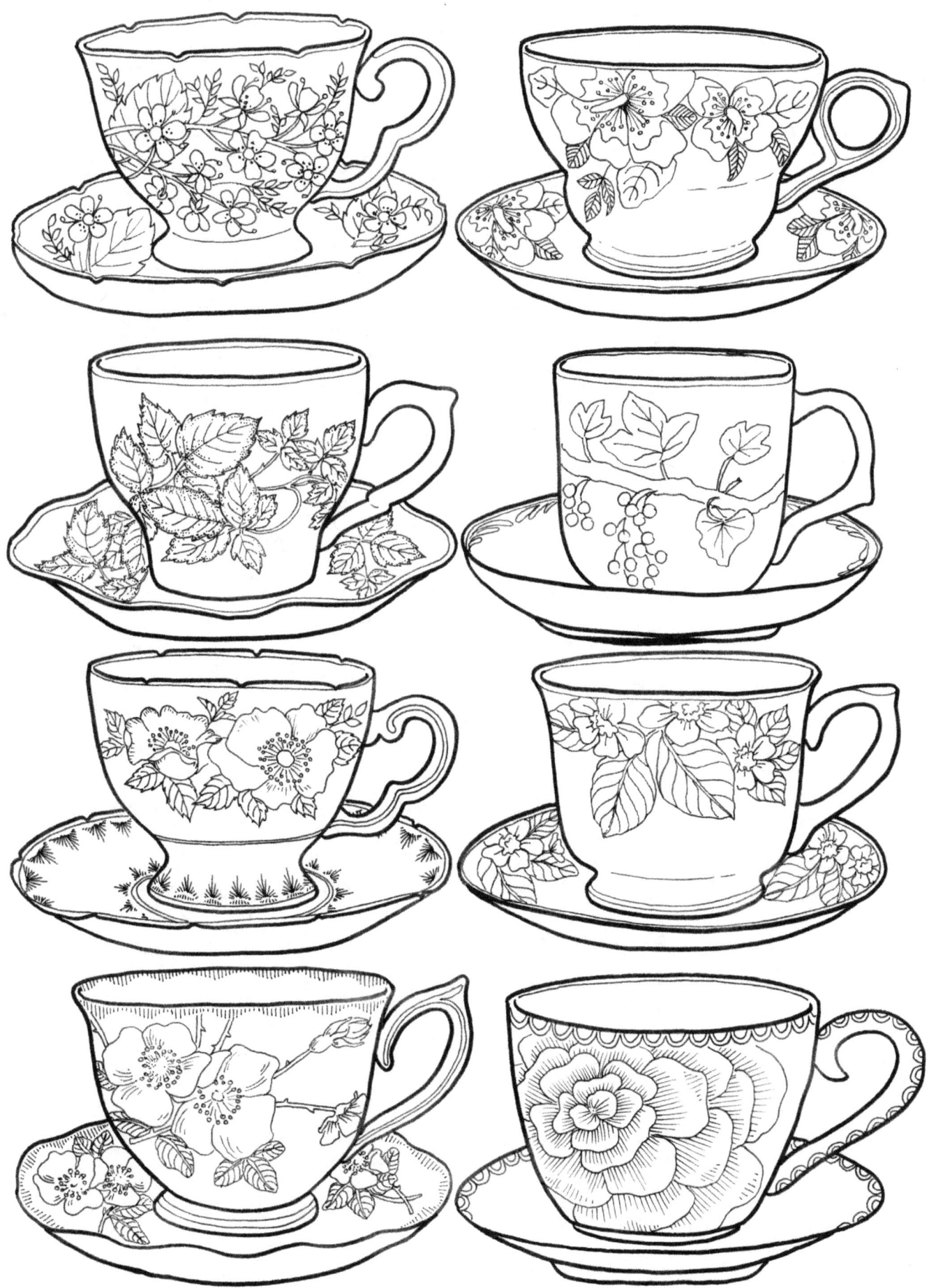

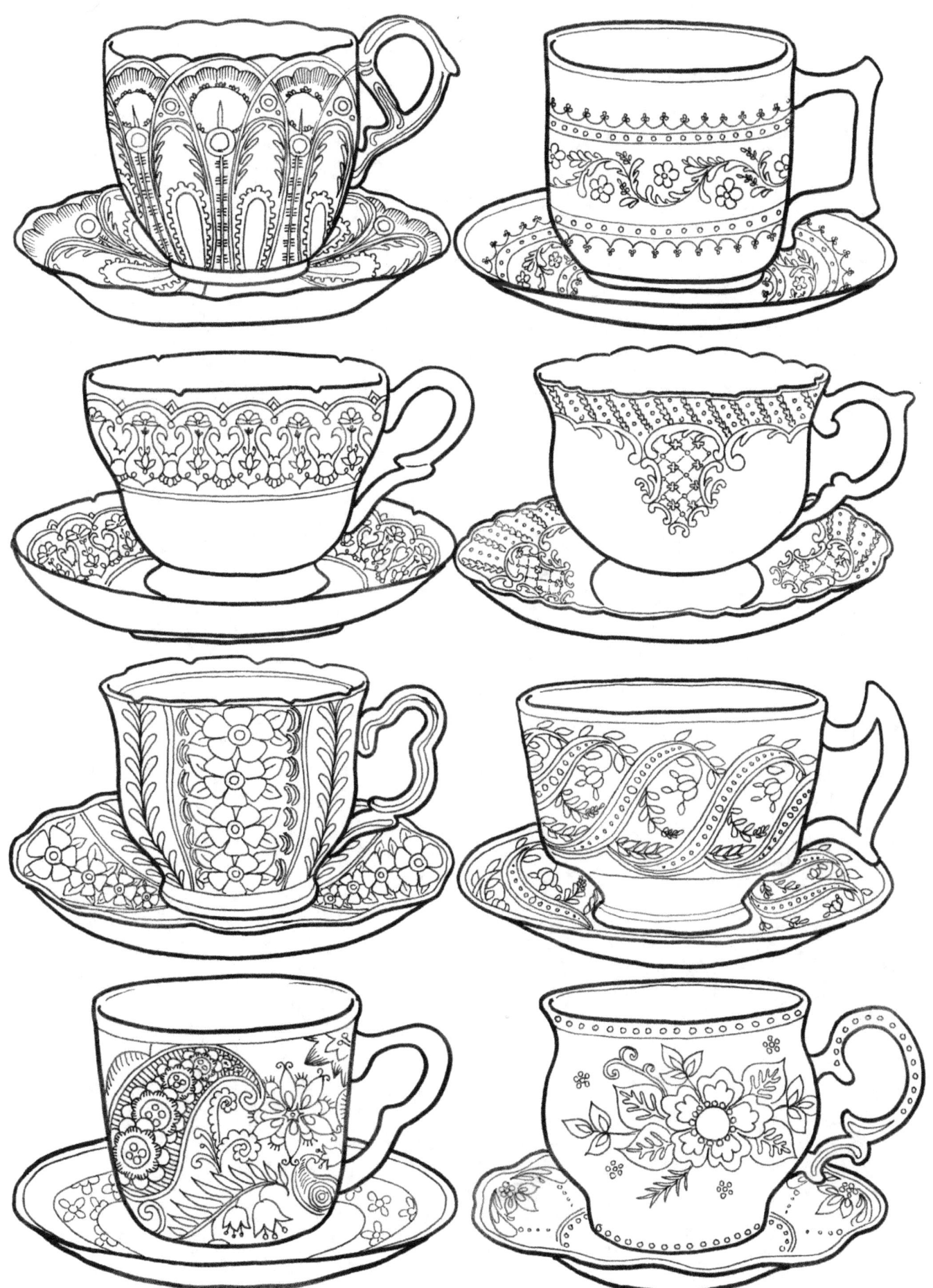

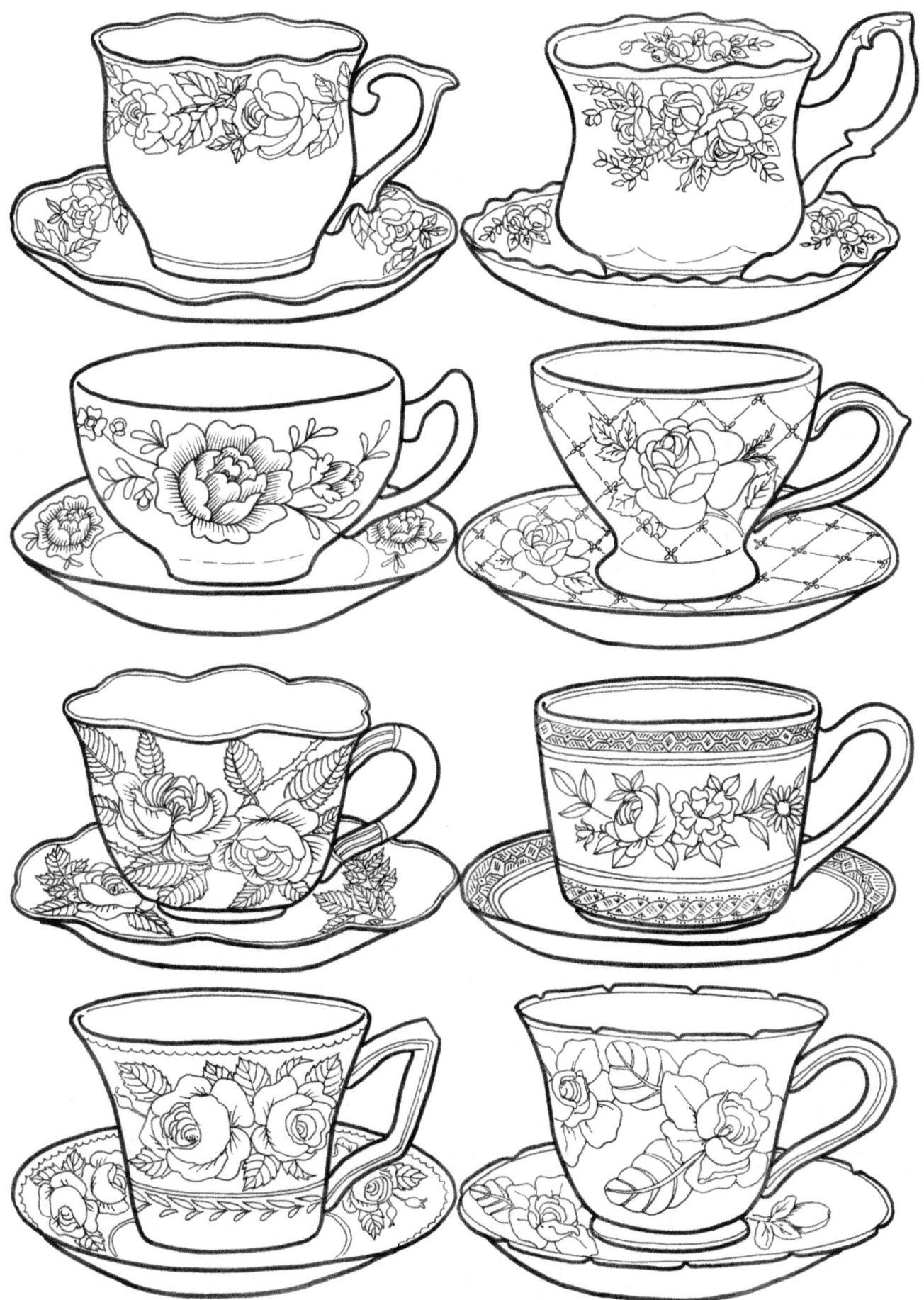

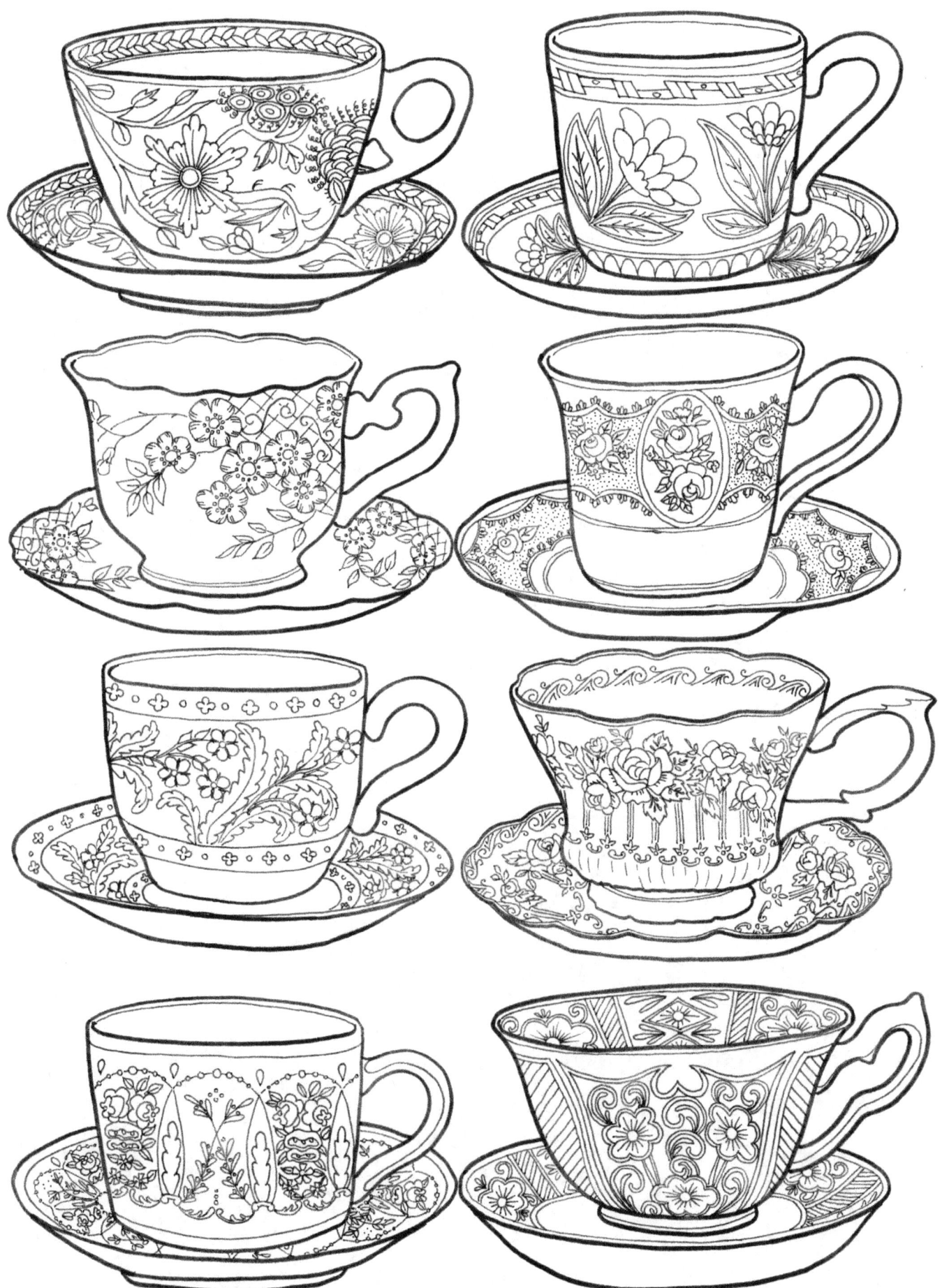

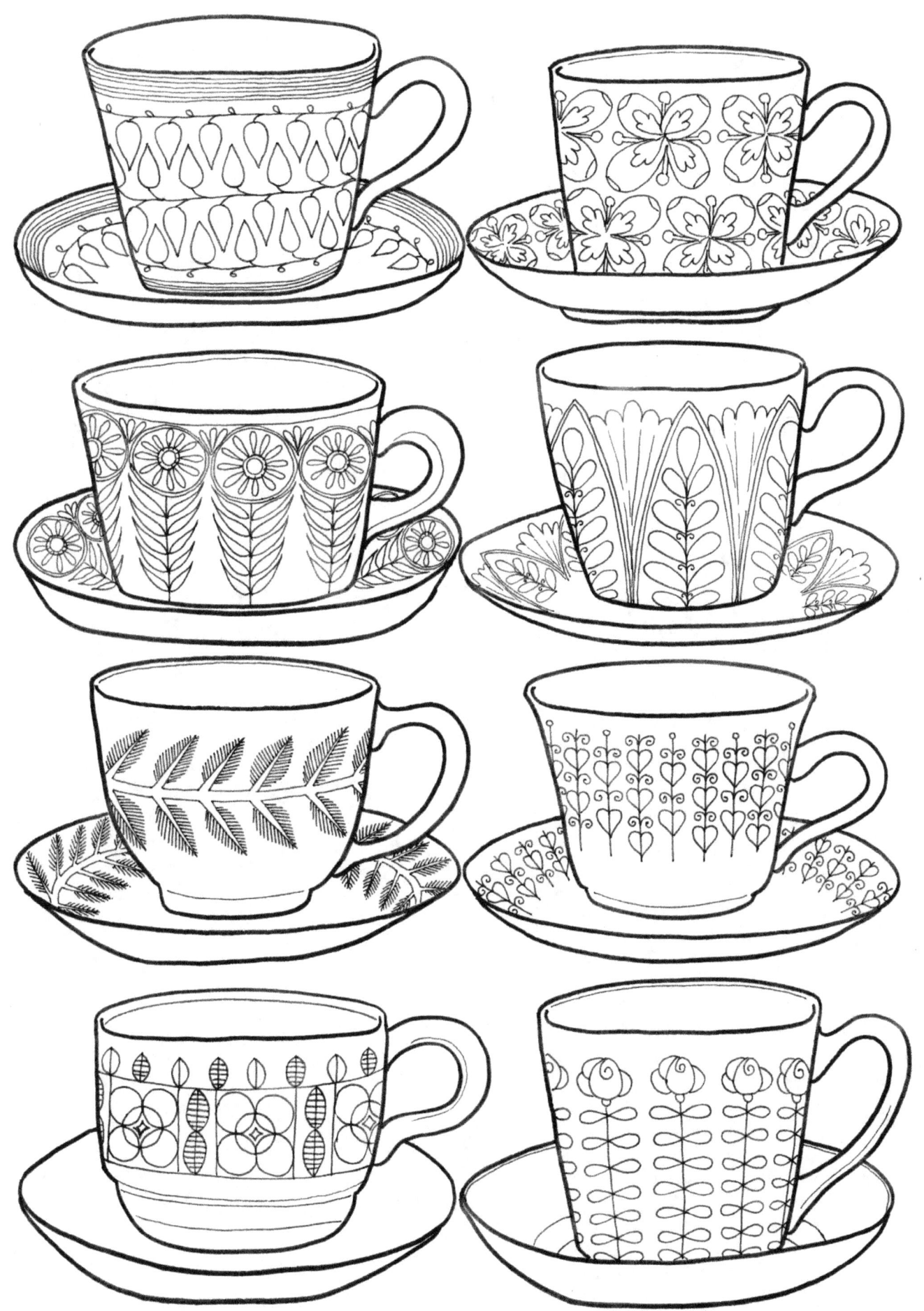

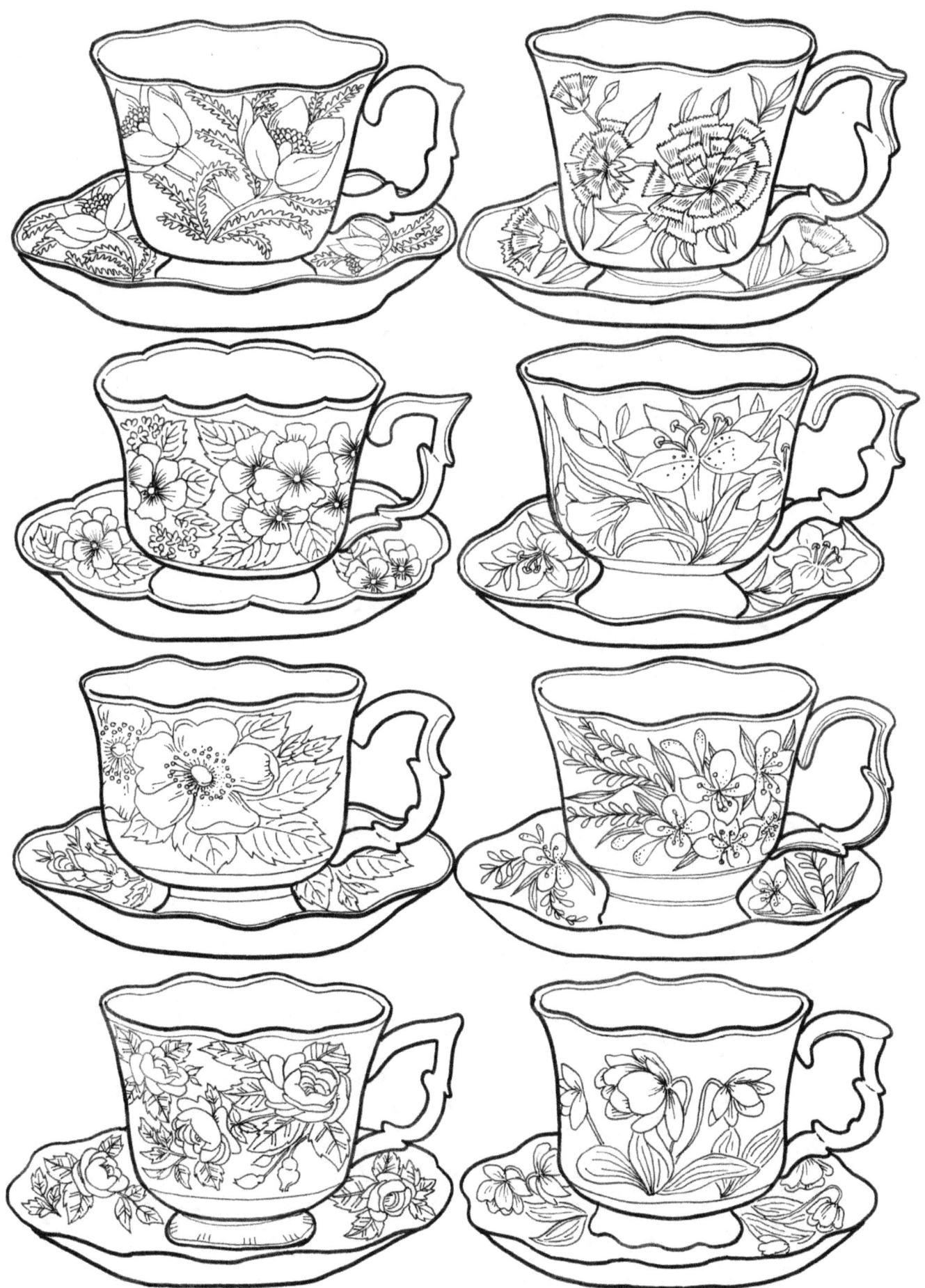

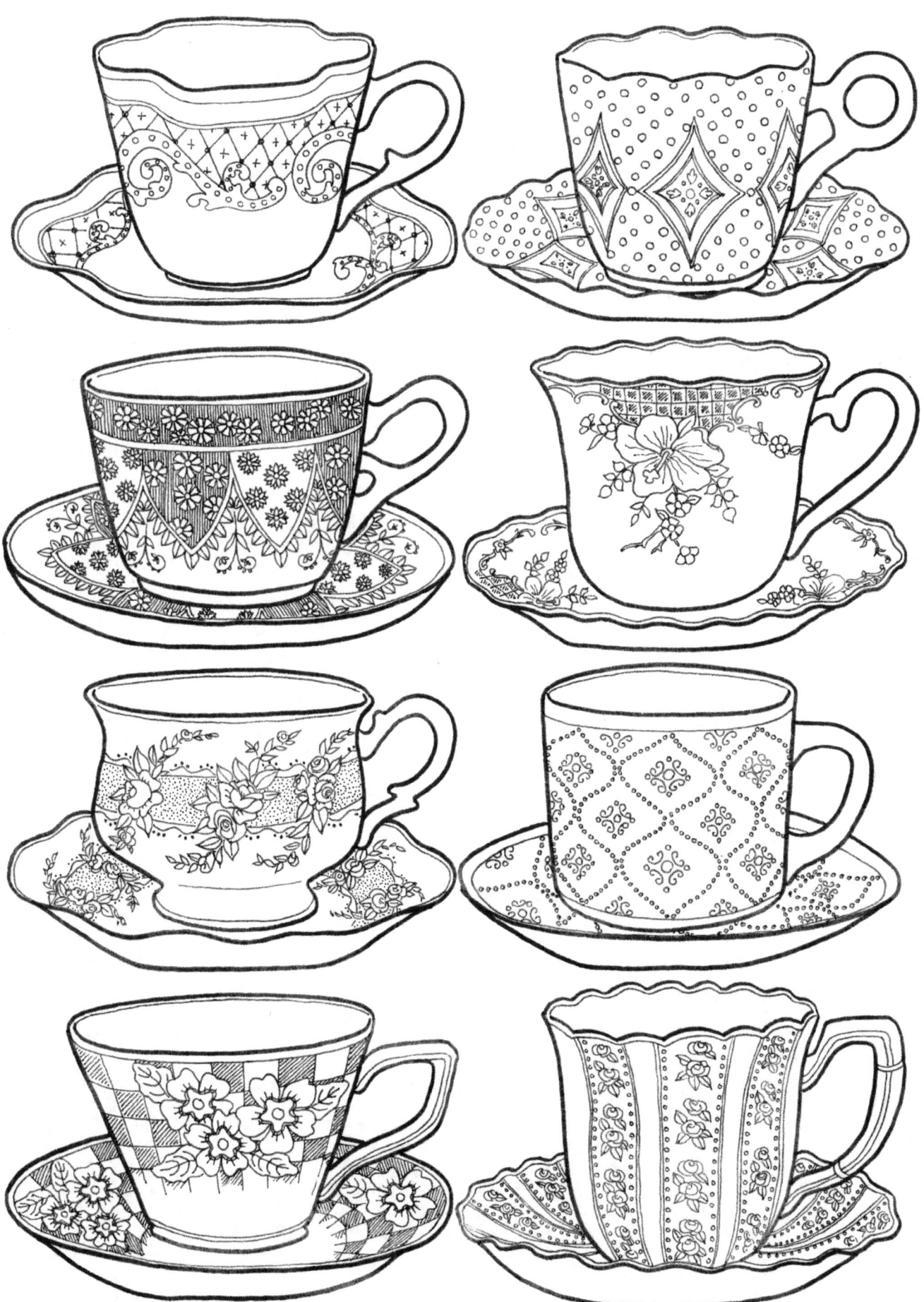

47

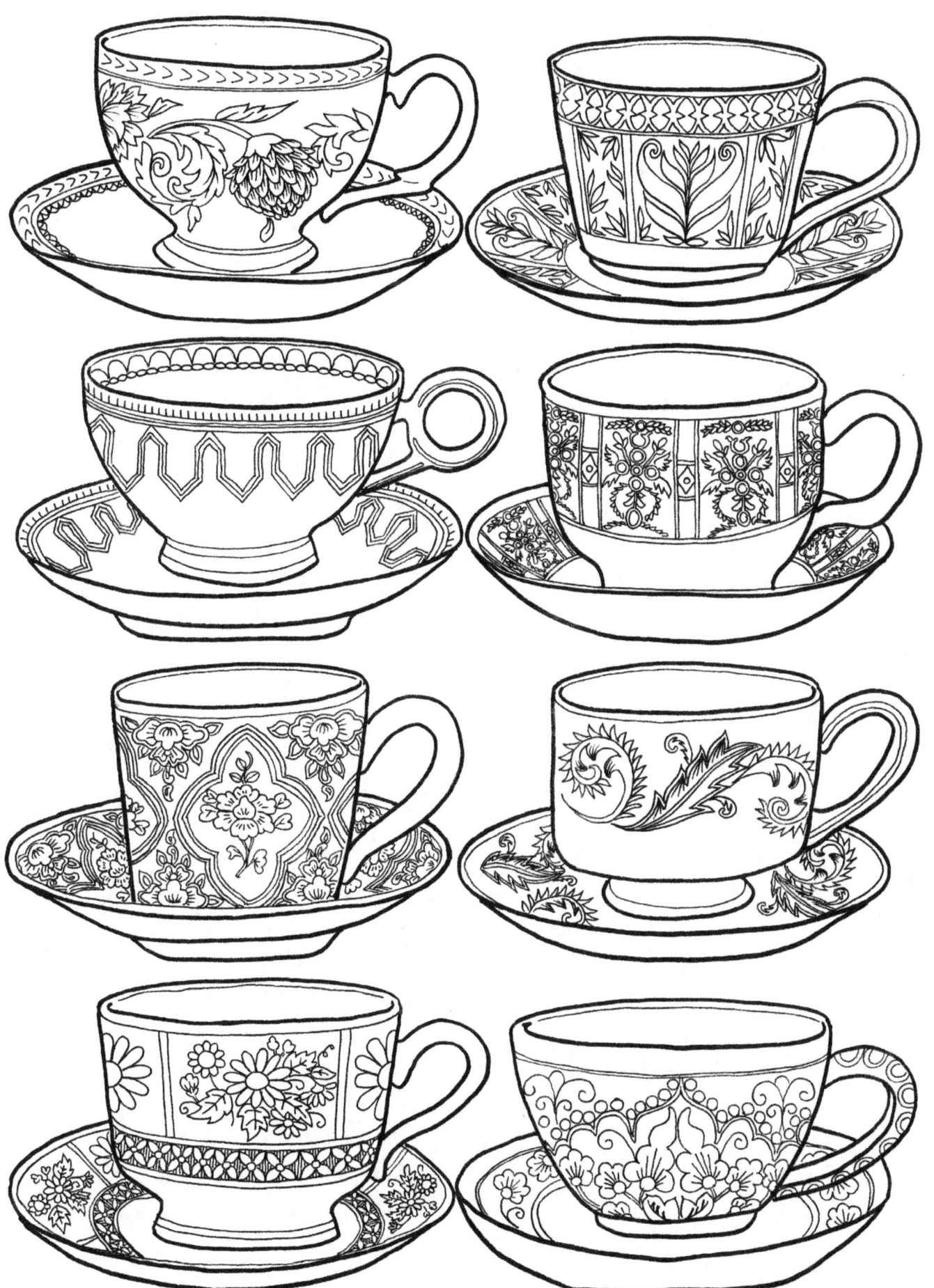